Coloring book for adults and kids airplane image for design

This coloring bookis belongs to

....

....

....

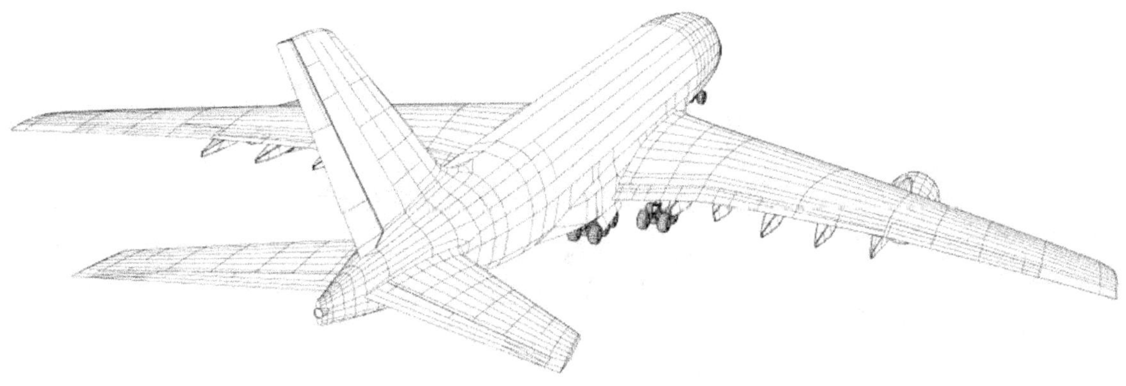

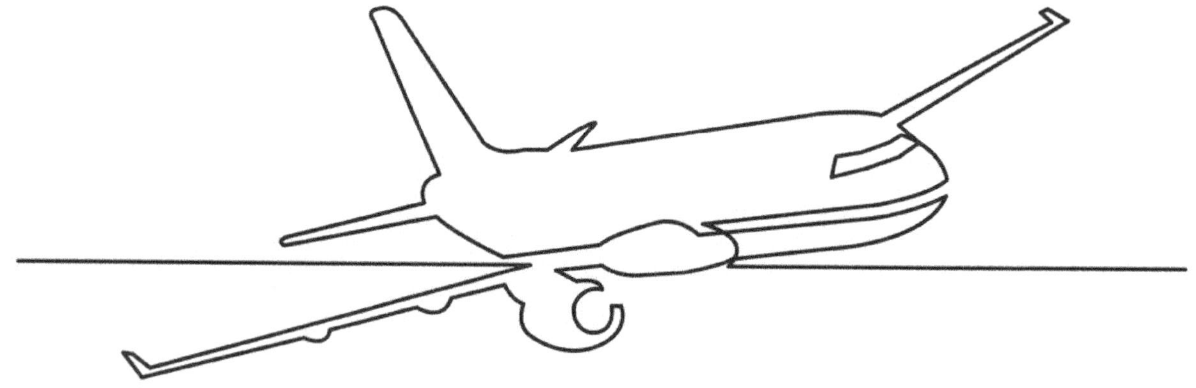

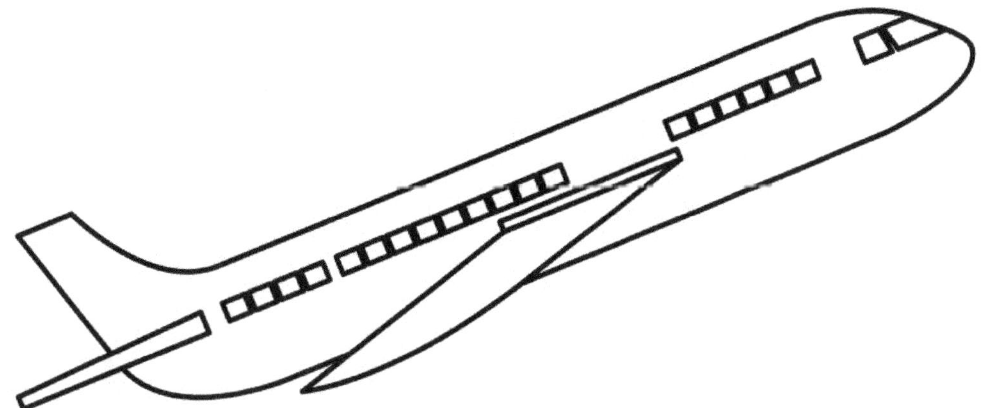

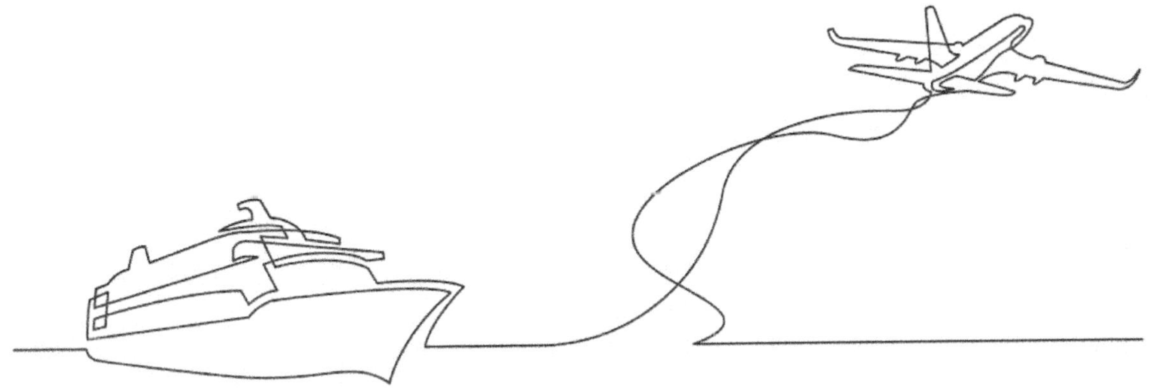

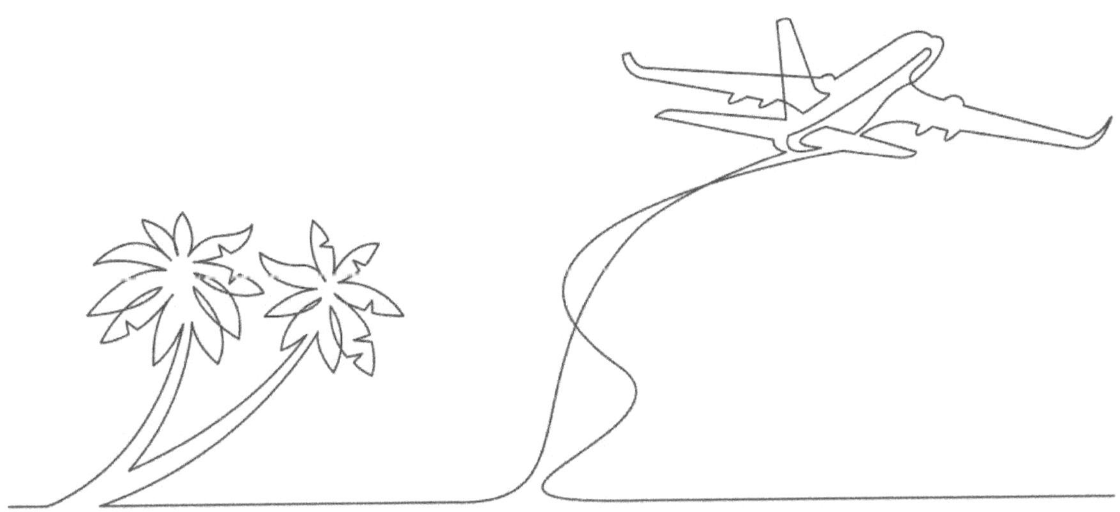

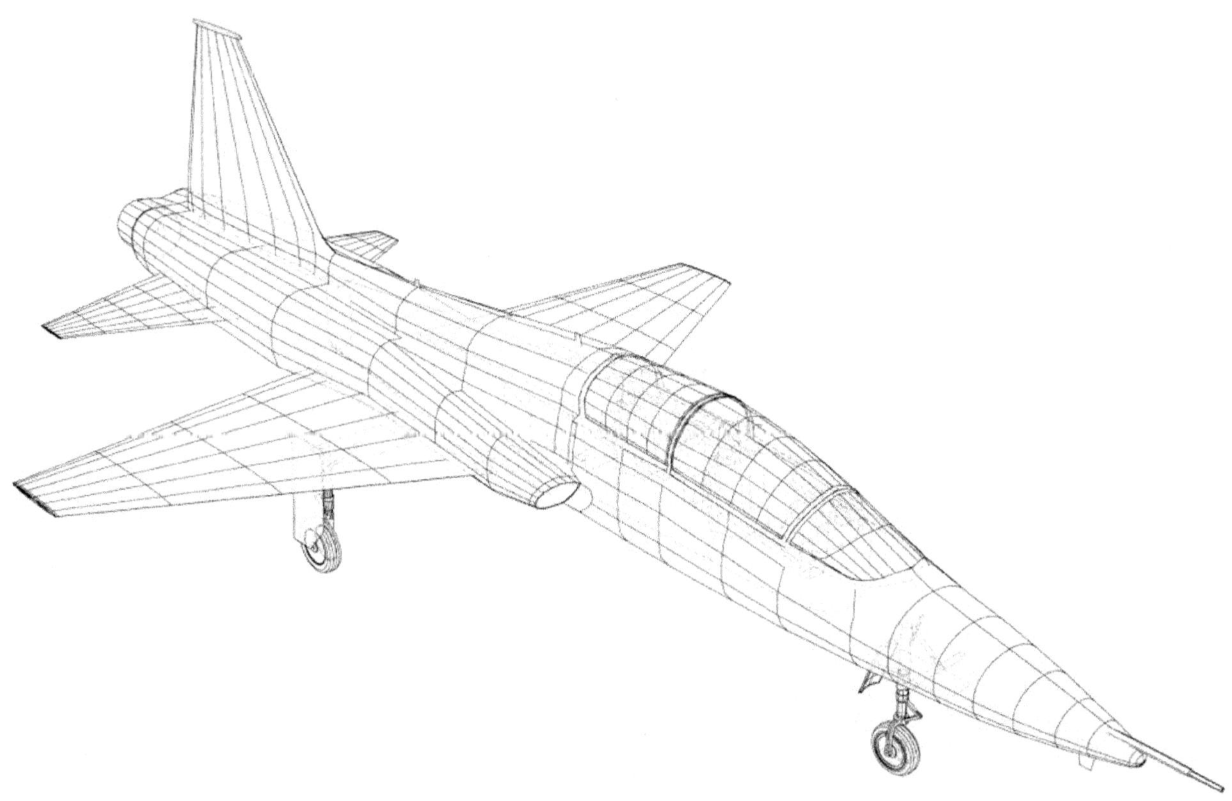

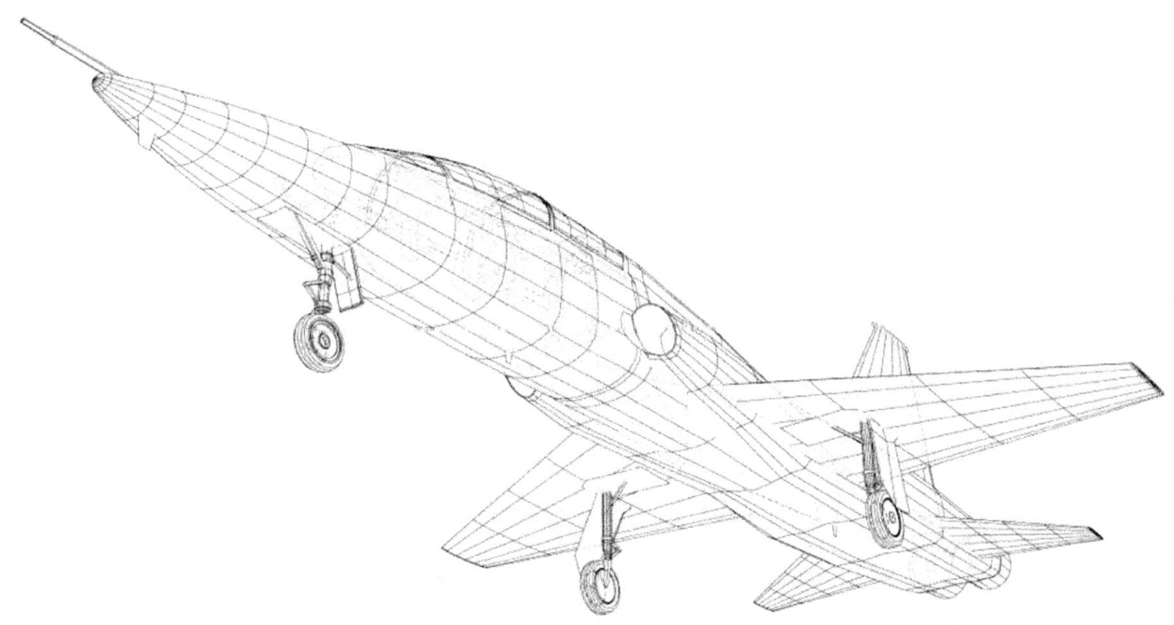

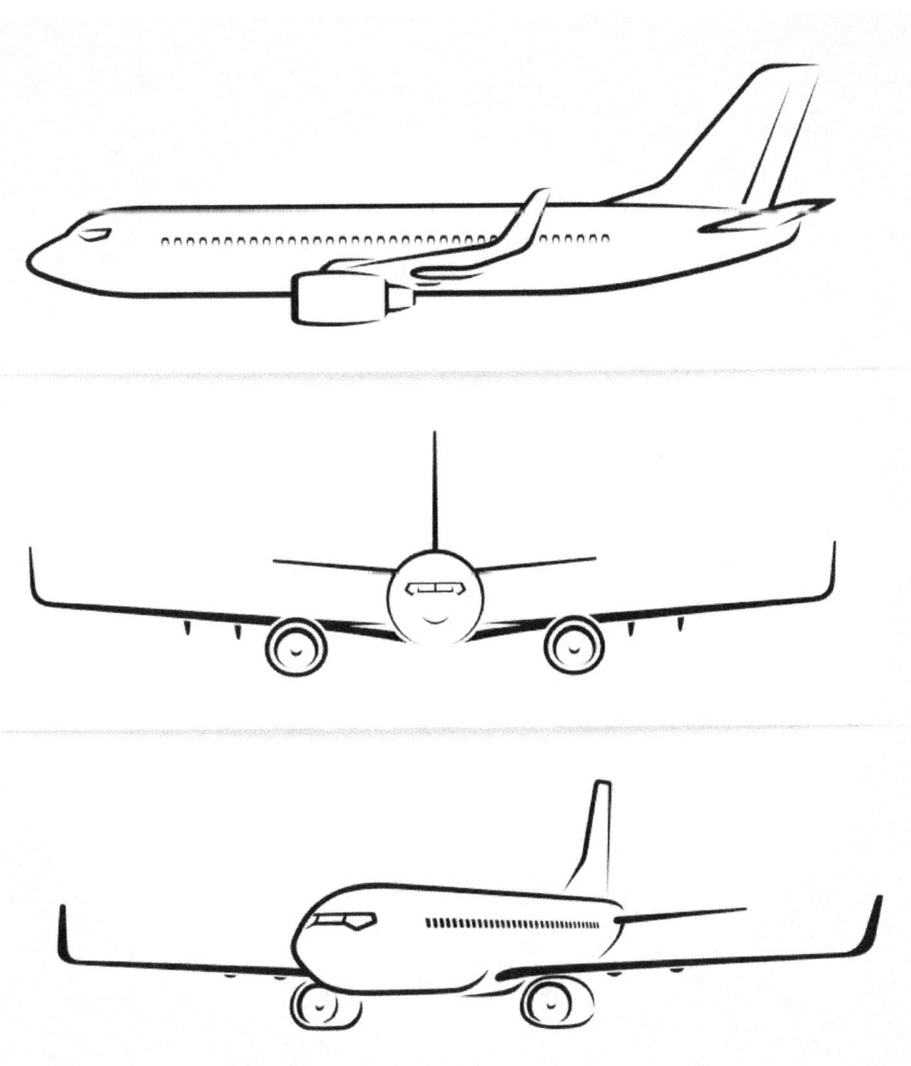

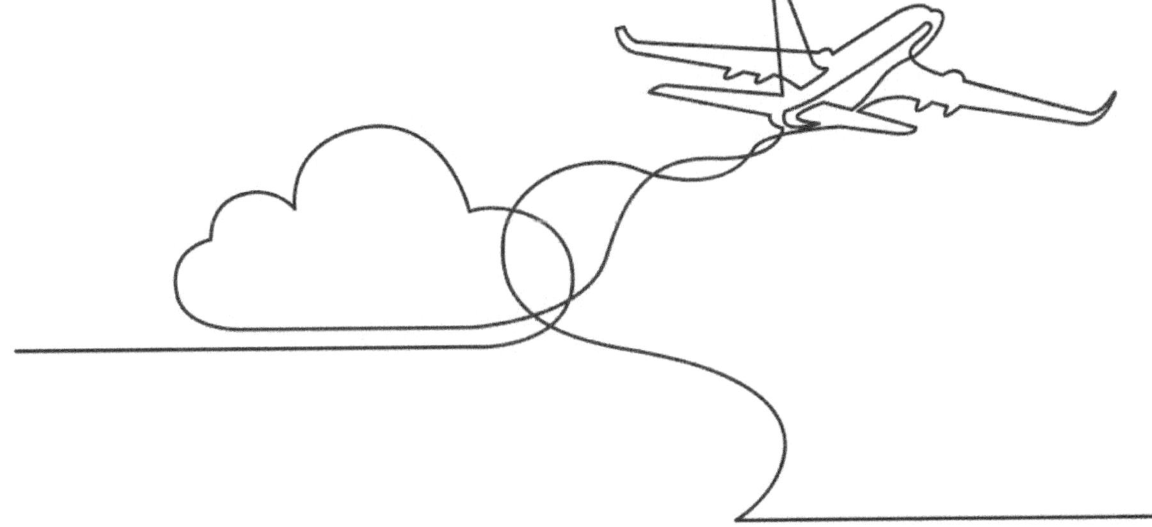

Let`s travel!

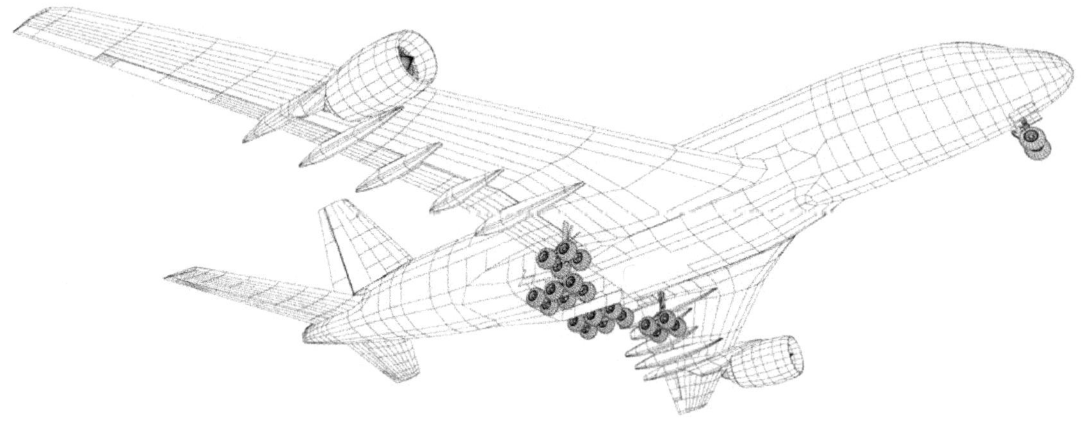

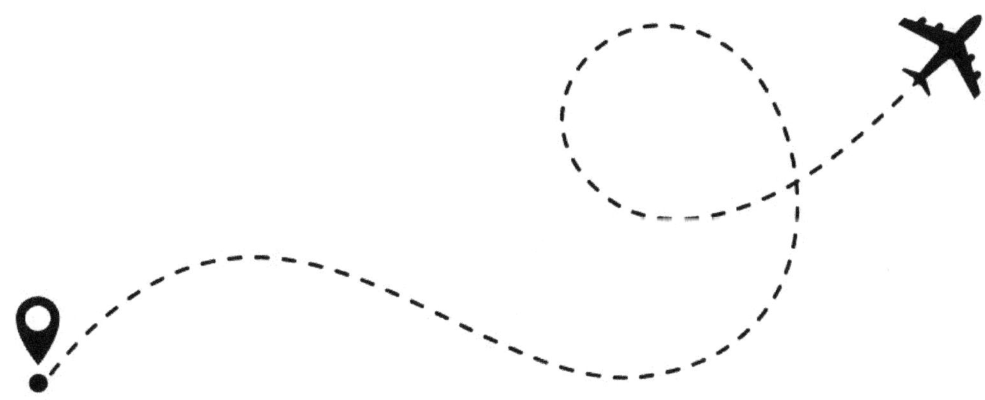

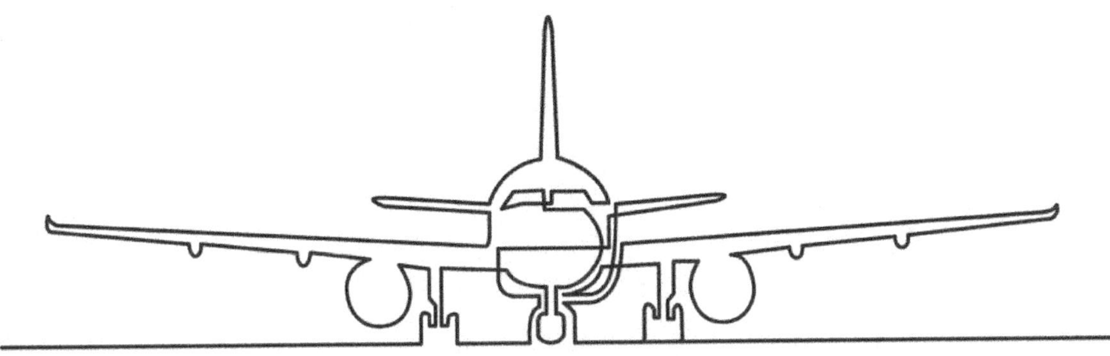

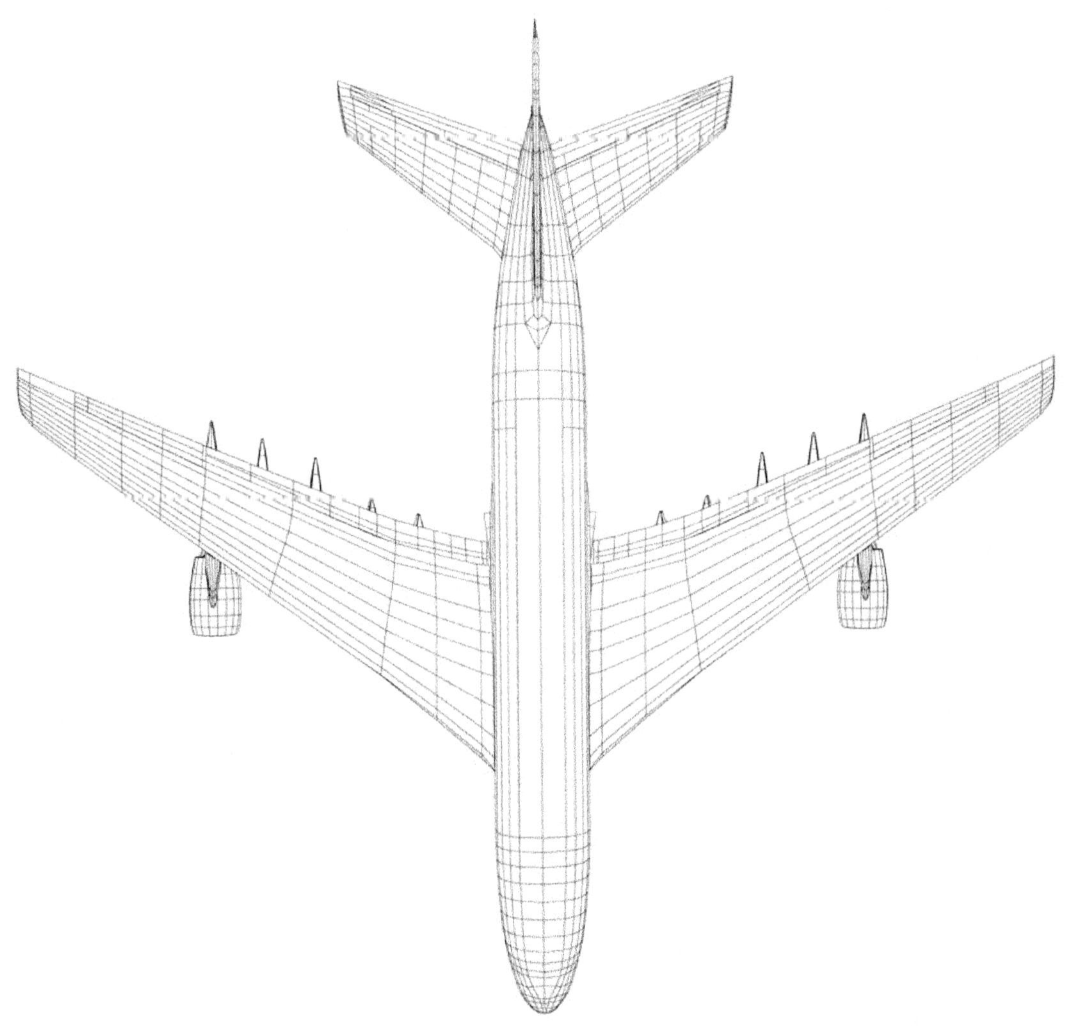

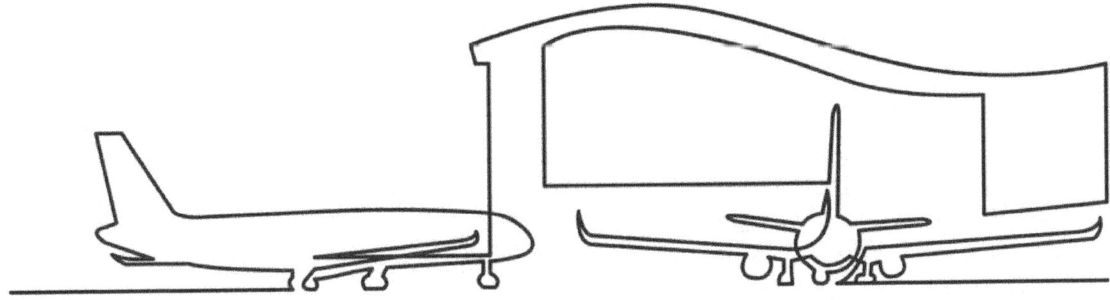

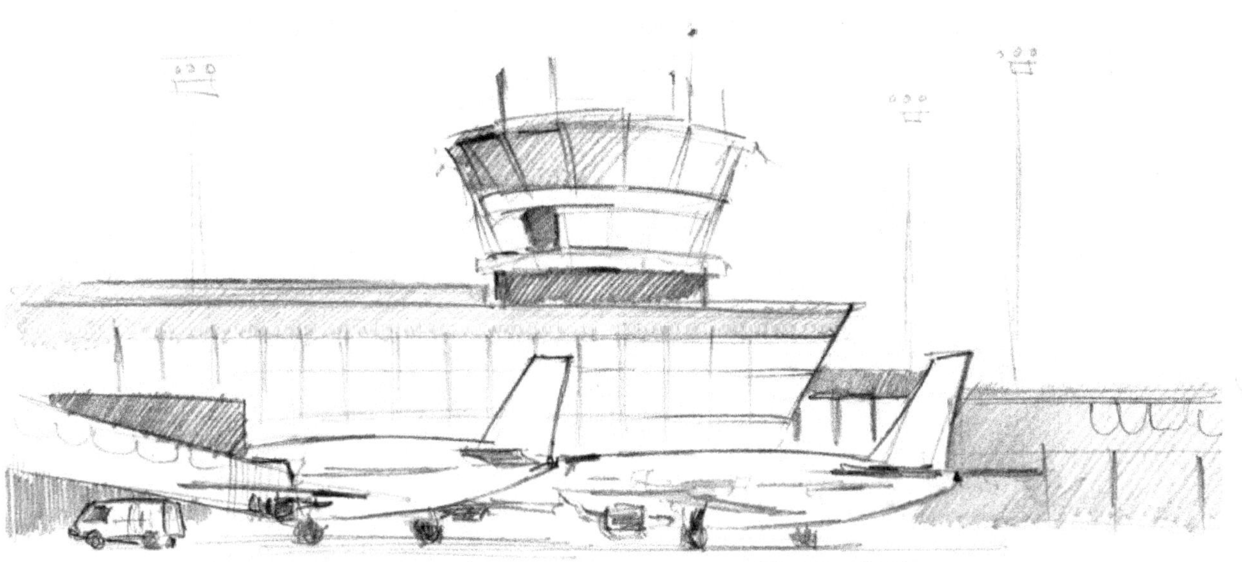

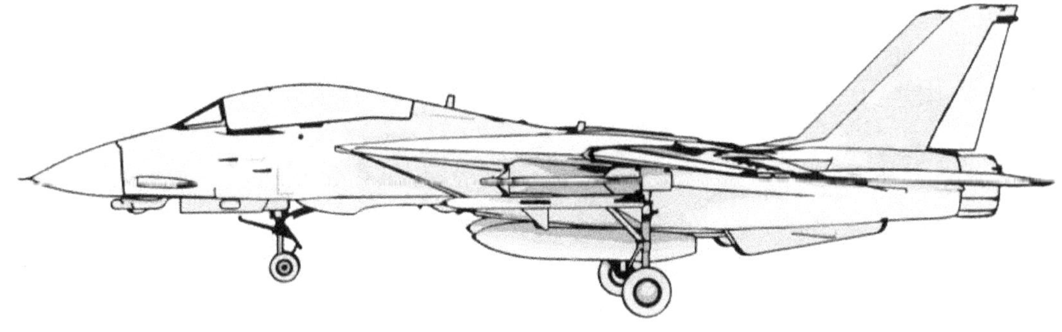

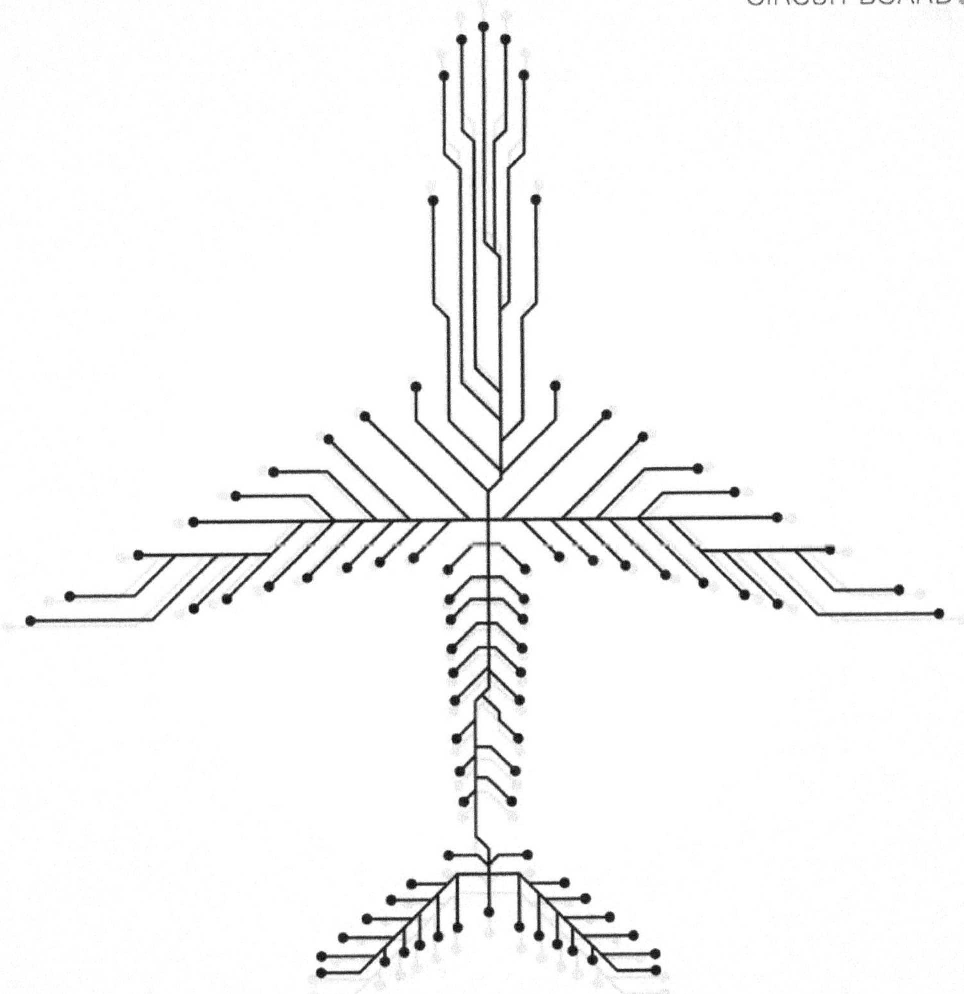

ABSTRACT AIRPLANE
CIRCUIT BOARD VECTOR

be happy

AIRPORT

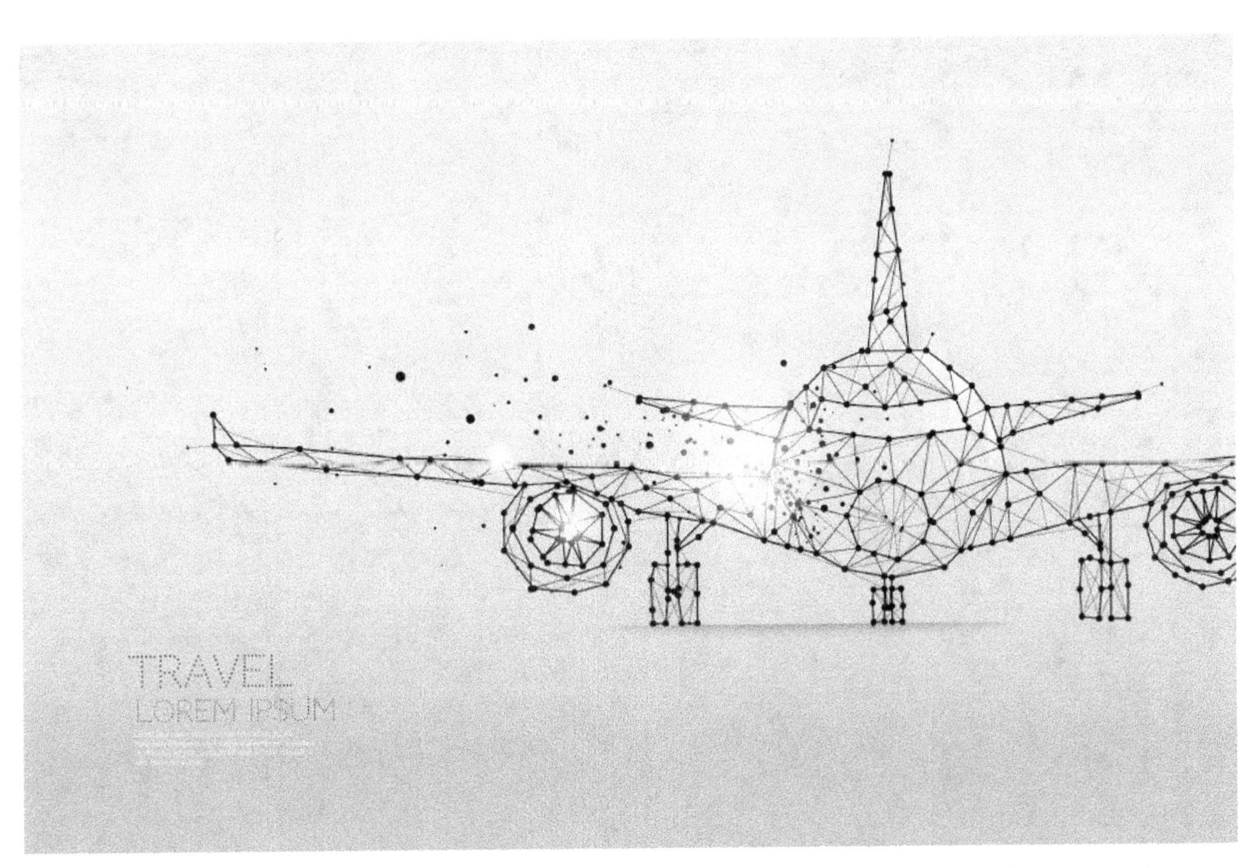
TRAVEL
LOREM IPSUM

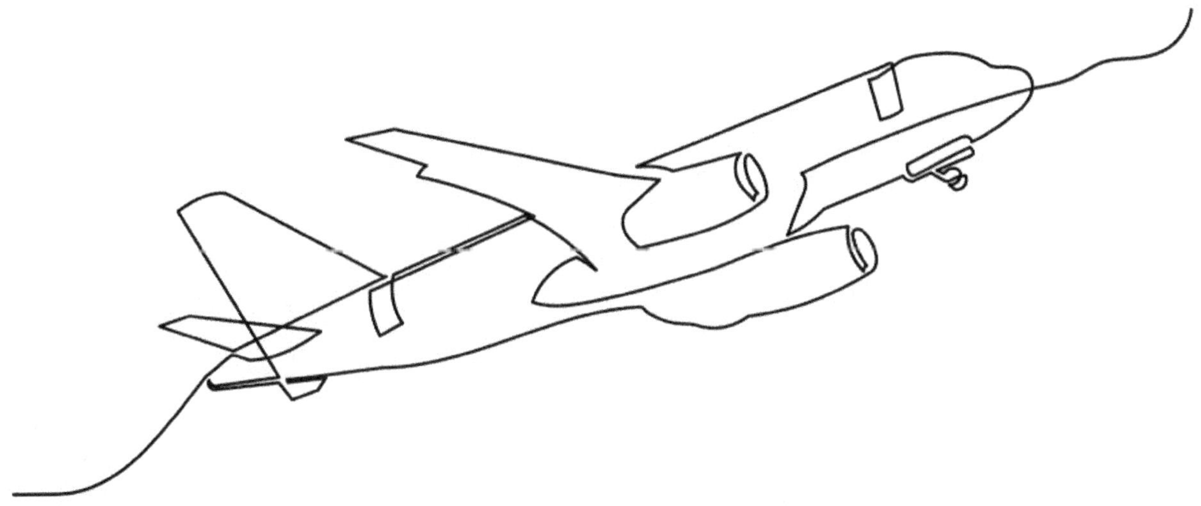